APOCALYPSE
COLORING BOOK

COLOR UNTIL THE VERY END!

Racehorse Publishing

Racehorse Publishing books may be purchased in bulk at special discounts for sales promotion, corporate gifts, fund-raising, or educational purposes. Special editions can also be created to specifications. For details, contact the Special Sales Department, Skyhorse Publishing, 307 West 36th Street, 11th Floor, New York, NY 10018 or info@skyhorsepublishing.com.

Racehorse Publishing™ is a pending trademark of Skyhorse Publishing, Inc.®, a Delaware corporation.

Visit our website at www.skyhorsepublishing.com.

10 9 8 7 6 5 4 3 2

Cover design, illustration,
and interior artwork by Ted Rechlin

Print ISBN: 978-1-944686-90-1

Printed in the United States of America

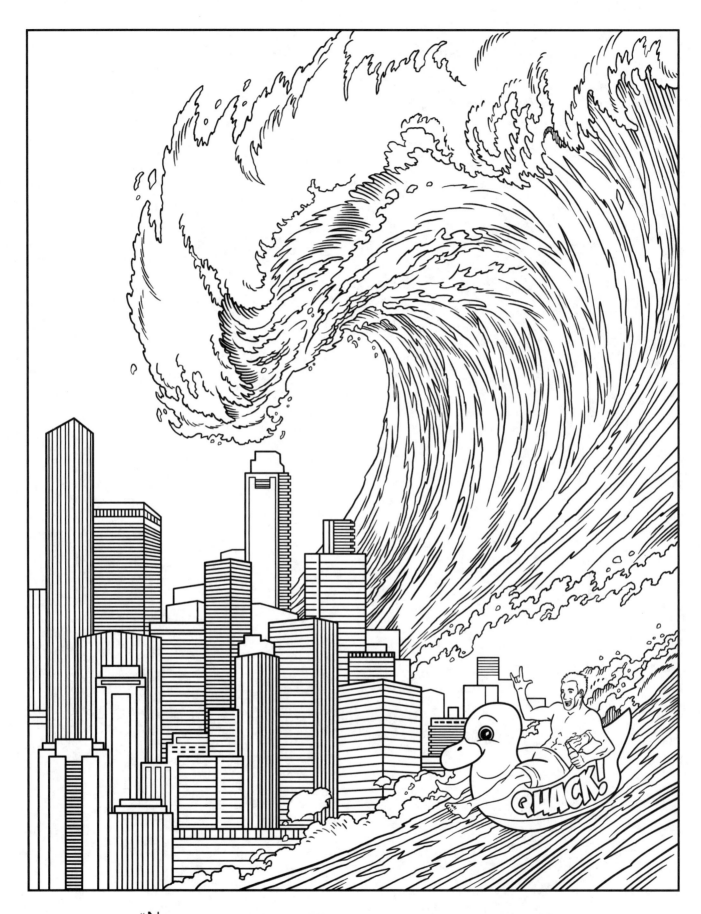

"NEVER GIVE UP, FOR THAT IS JUST THE PLACE AND TIME
THAT THE TIDE WILL TURN." —HARRIET BEECHER STOWE

1

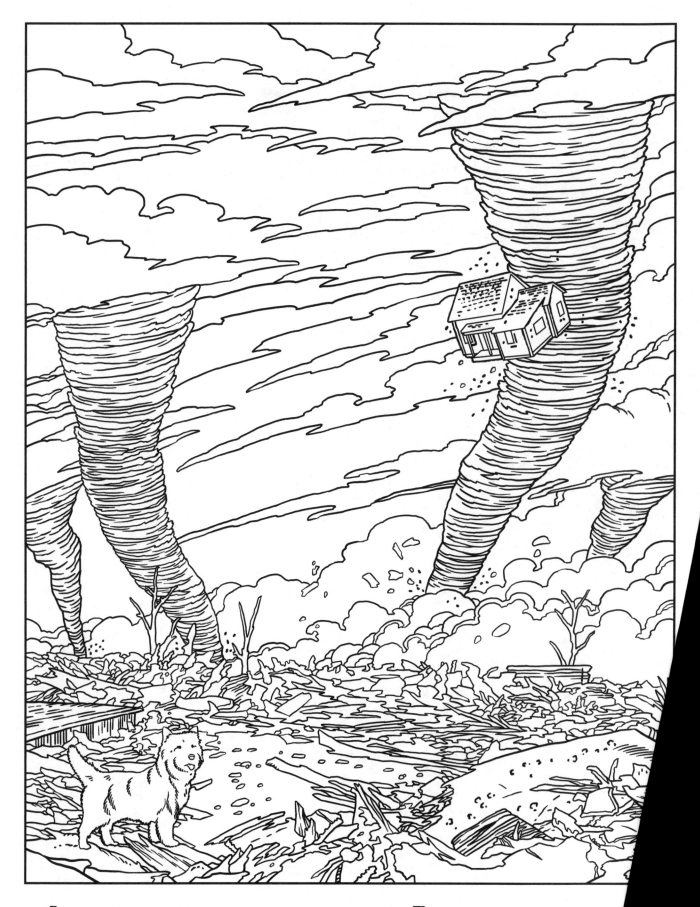

"Be thou the rainbow in the storms of life. The evening beam that s͟m͟[...] the clouds away, and tints tomorrow with prophetic ray."—Lord B[...]

MILES

YRON

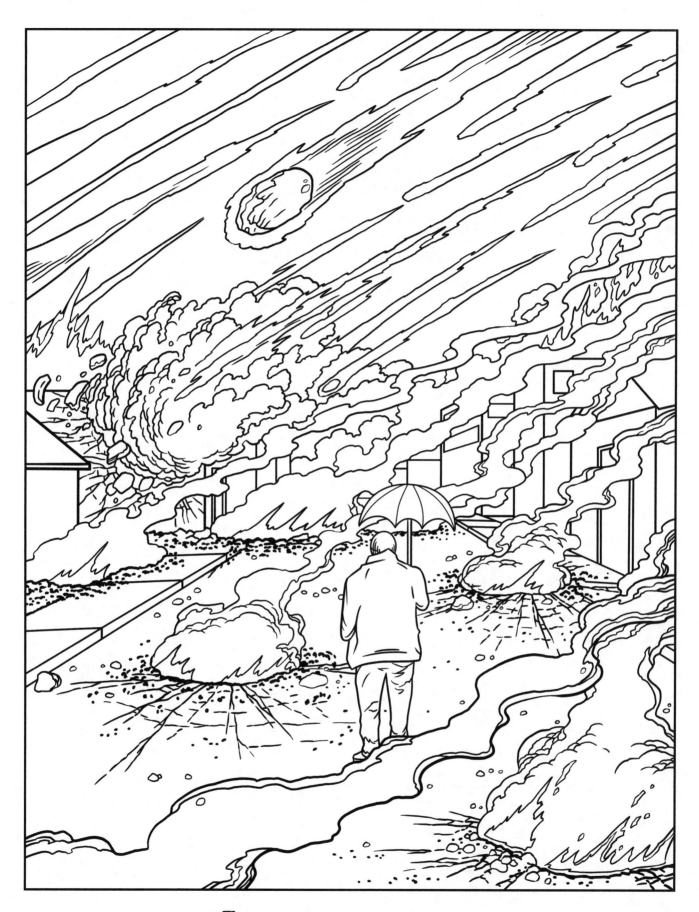

"That it will never come again
is what makes life so sweet."—Emily Dickinson

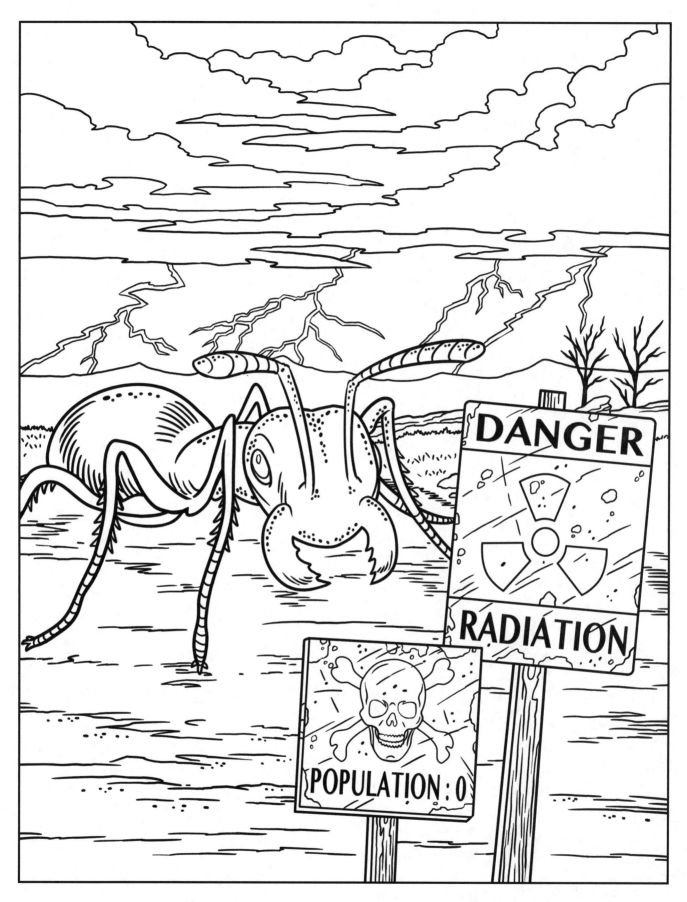

"I KNOW NOT ALL THAT MAY BE COMING,
BUT BE IT WHAT IT WILL, I'LL GO TO IT LAUGHING." —HERMAN MELVILLE

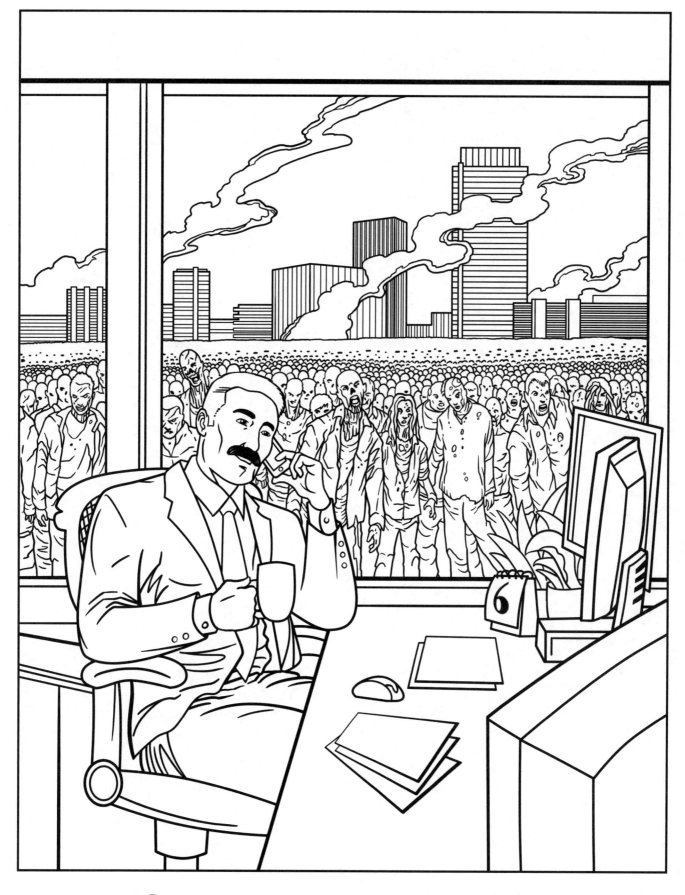

"COURAGE IS KNOWING WHAT NOT TO FEAR." —PLATO

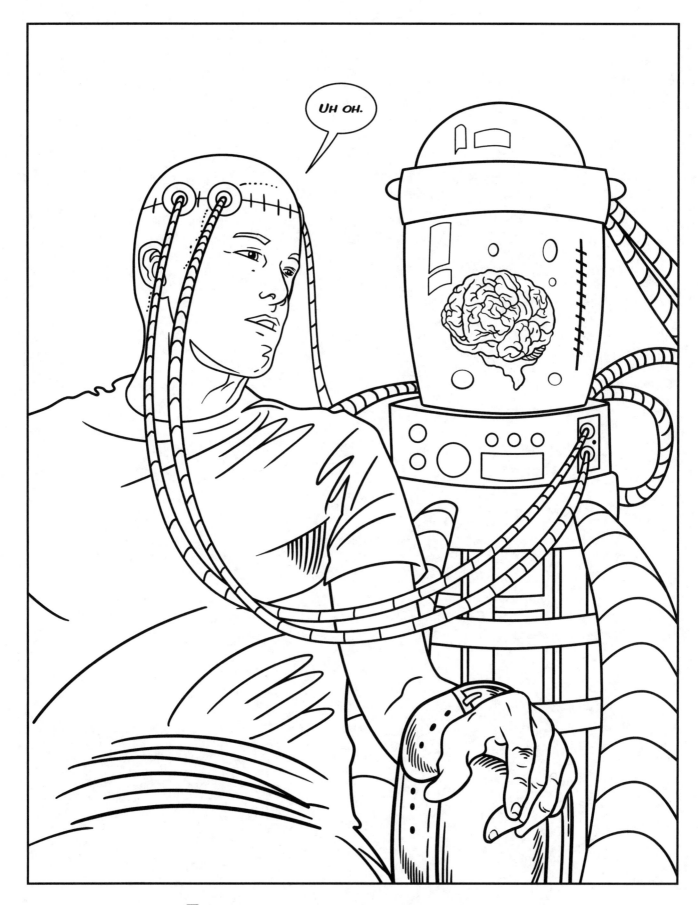

"The future belongs to those who believe in the beauty of their dreams." —Eleanor Roosevelt

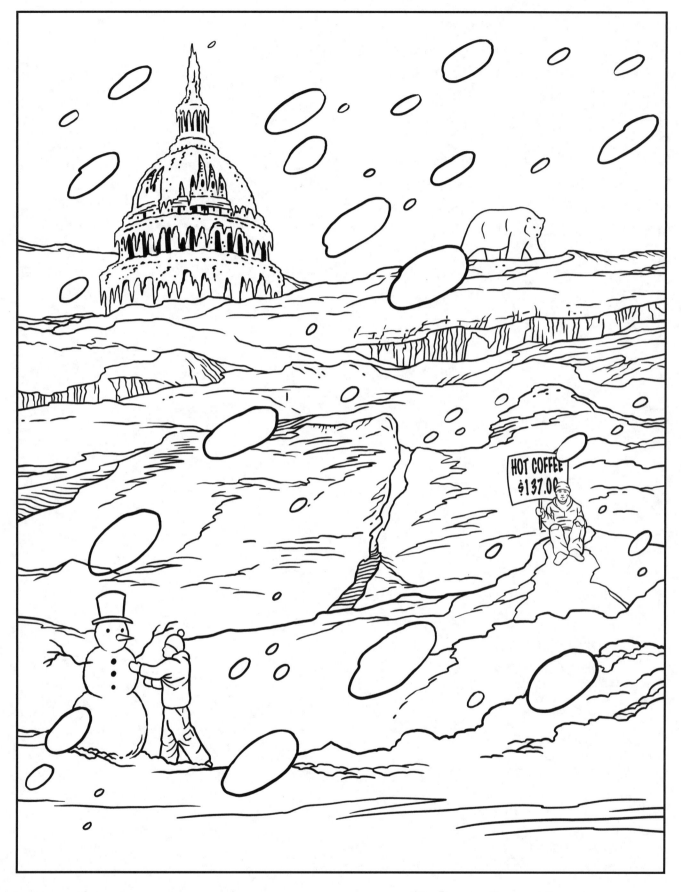

"IF WINTER COMES, CAN SPRING BE FAR BEHIND?"—PERCY BYSHE SHELLEY

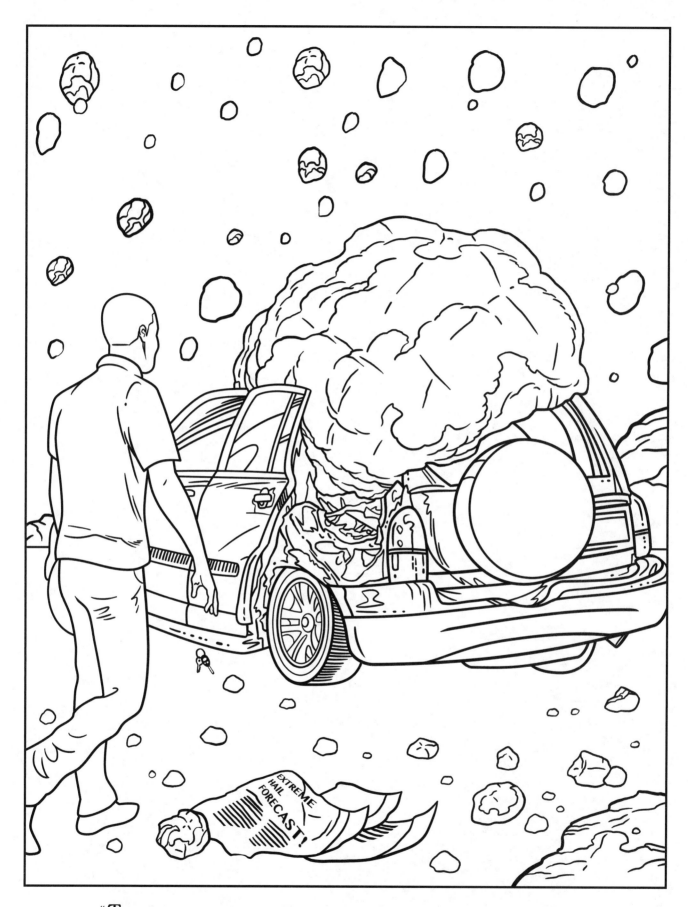

"The first and final thing you have to do in this world is to last it and not be smashed by it."—Ernest Hemingway

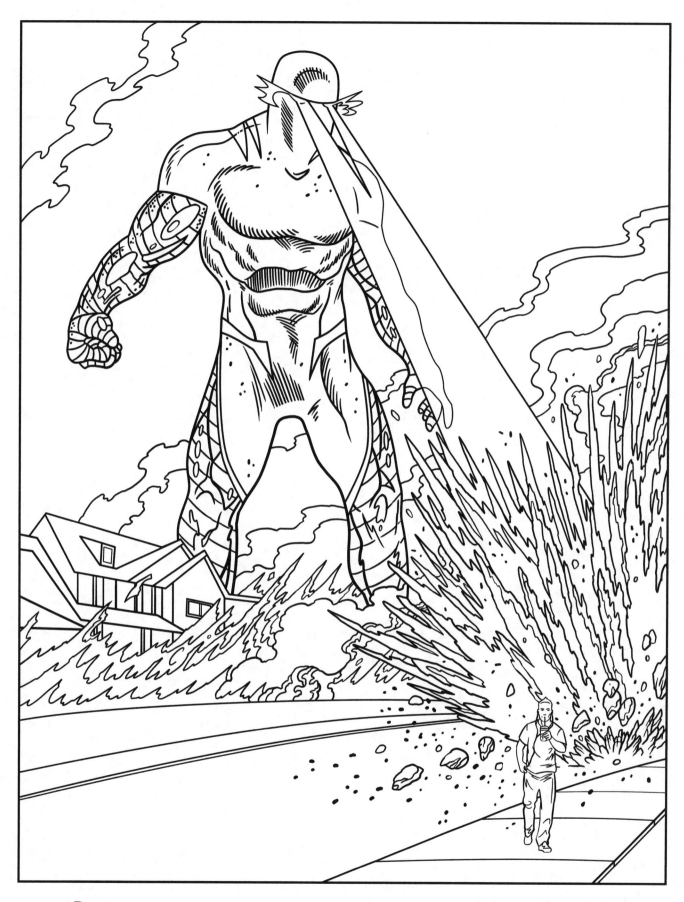

"DON'T CRY BECAUSE IT'S OVER, SMILE BECAUSE IT HAPPENED."—DR. SEUSS

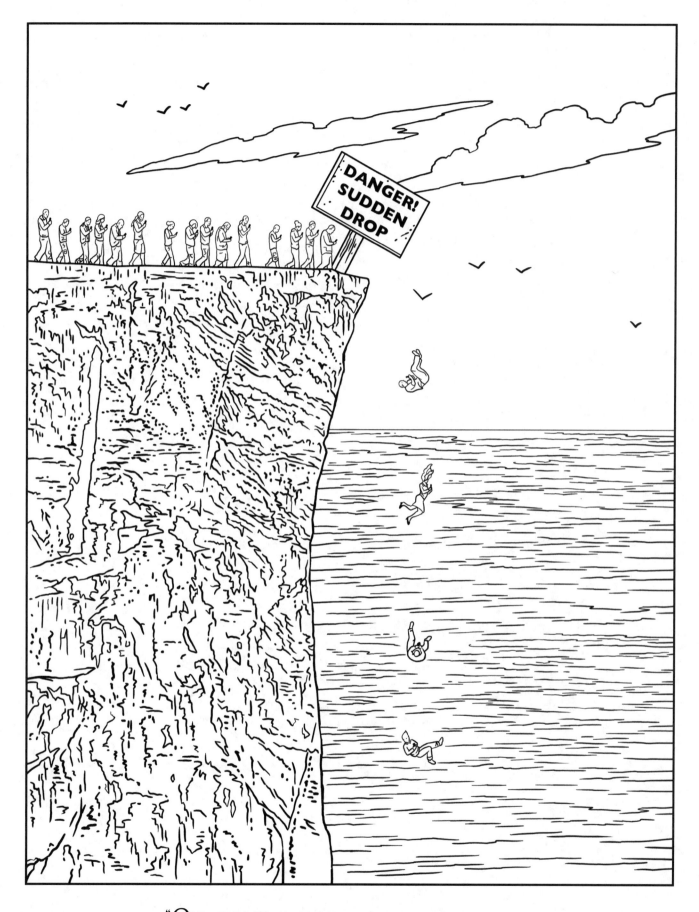

"OUR GREATEST GLORY IS NOT IN NEVER FALLING,
BUT IN RISING EVERY TIME WE FALL." —CONFUCIUS

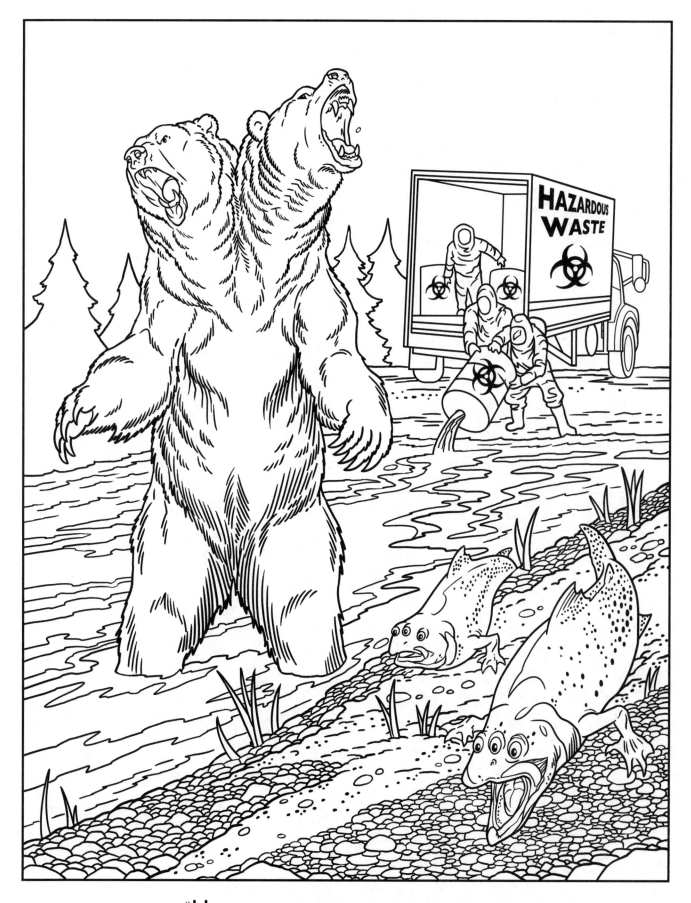

"HE WHO HAS A WHY TO LIVE CAN BEAR
ALMOST ANY HOW."—FRIEDRICH NIETZSCHE

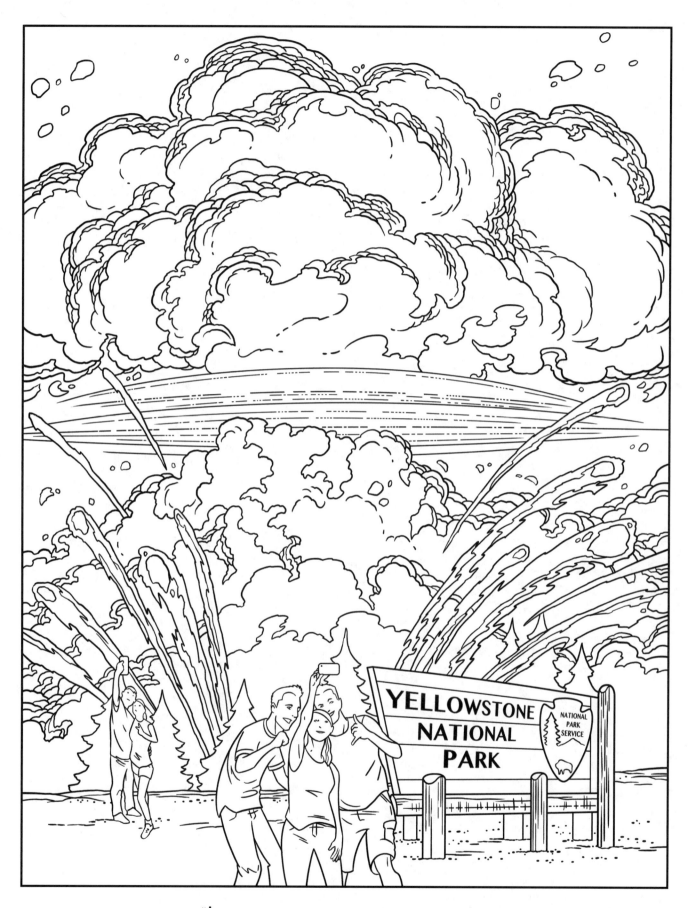

"If at every instant we may perish,
so at every instant we may be saved." —Jules Verne

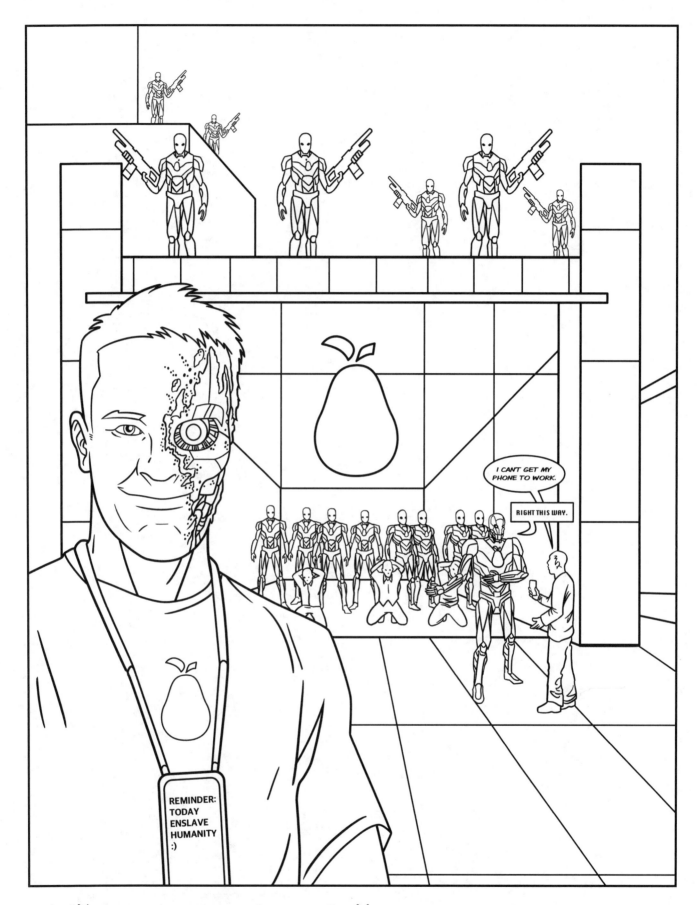

"Never let the future disturb you. You will meet it, if you have to, with the *same* weapons of reason which today arm you against the present." —Marcus Aurelius

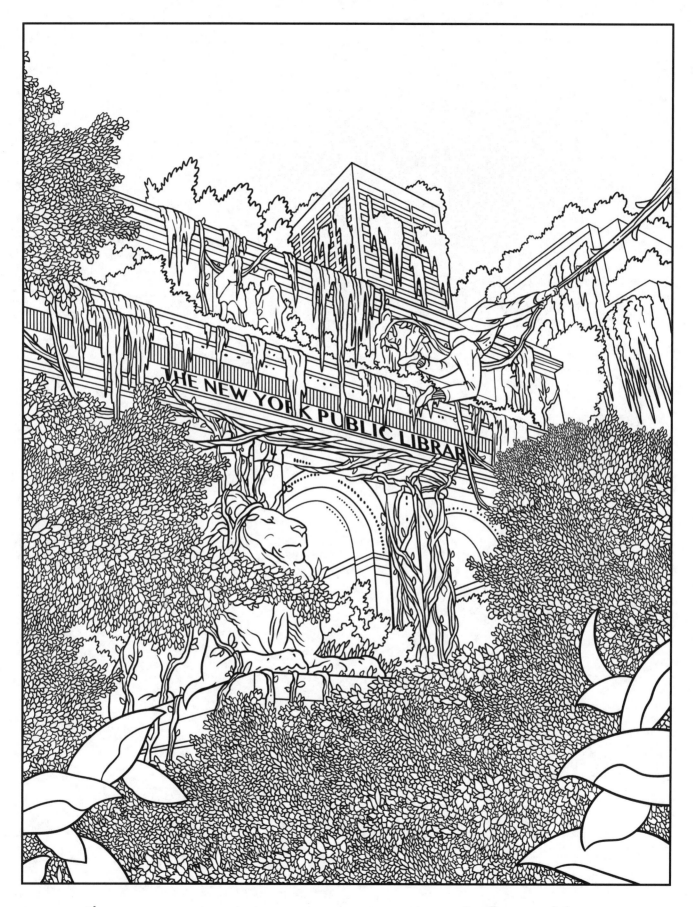

"I MUST HAVE FLOWERS, ALWAYS, AND ALWAYS."—CLAUDE MONET

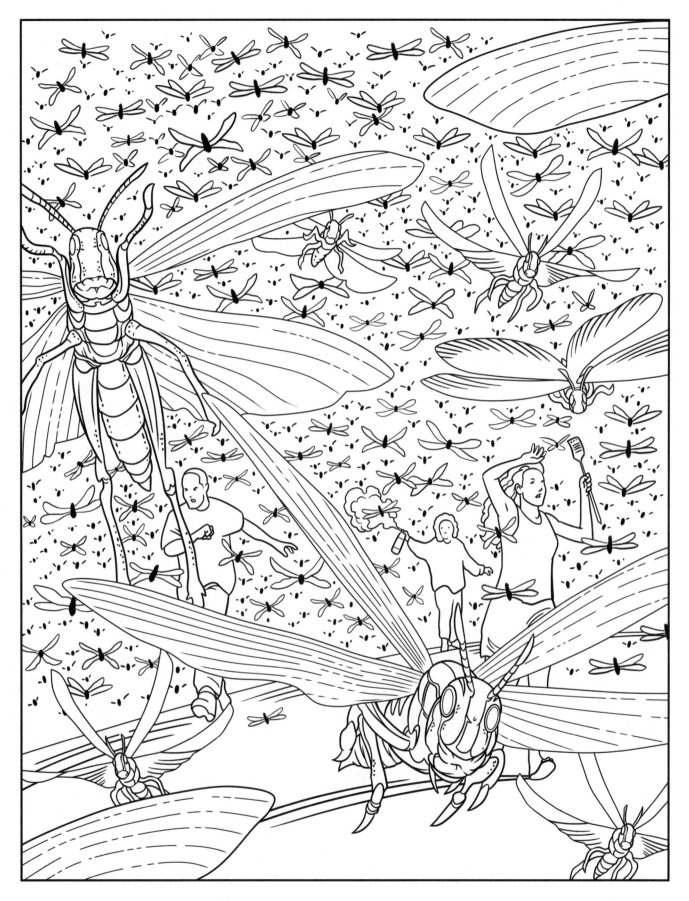

"YOU CAN'T WAIT FOR INSPIRATION.
YOU HAVE TO GO AFTER IT WITH A CLUB."—JACK LONDON

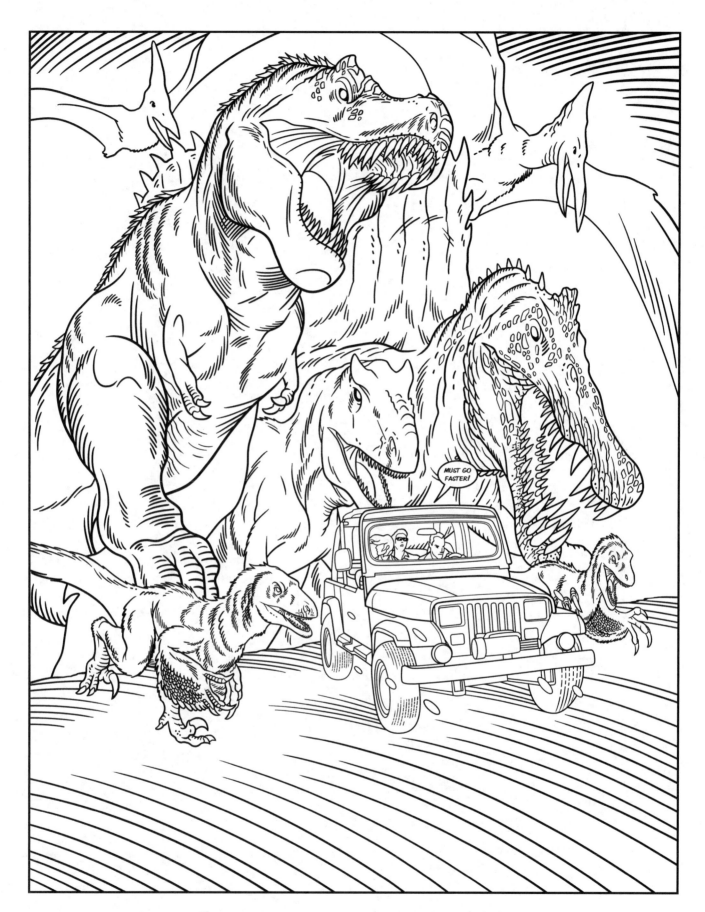

"I LIKE THE DREAMS OF THE FUTURE BETTER
THAN THE HISTORY OF THE PAST."—THOMAS JEFFERSON

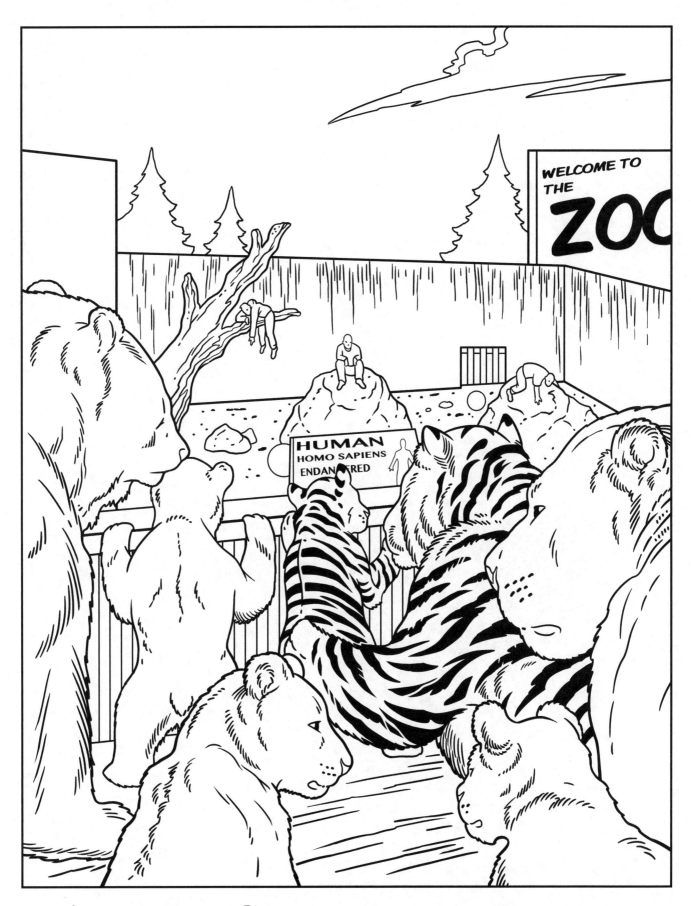

"LOVE THE ANIMALS: GOD HAS GIVEN THEM THE RUDIMENTS OF THOUGHT AND JOY UNTROUBLED." —FYODOR DOSTOYEVSKY

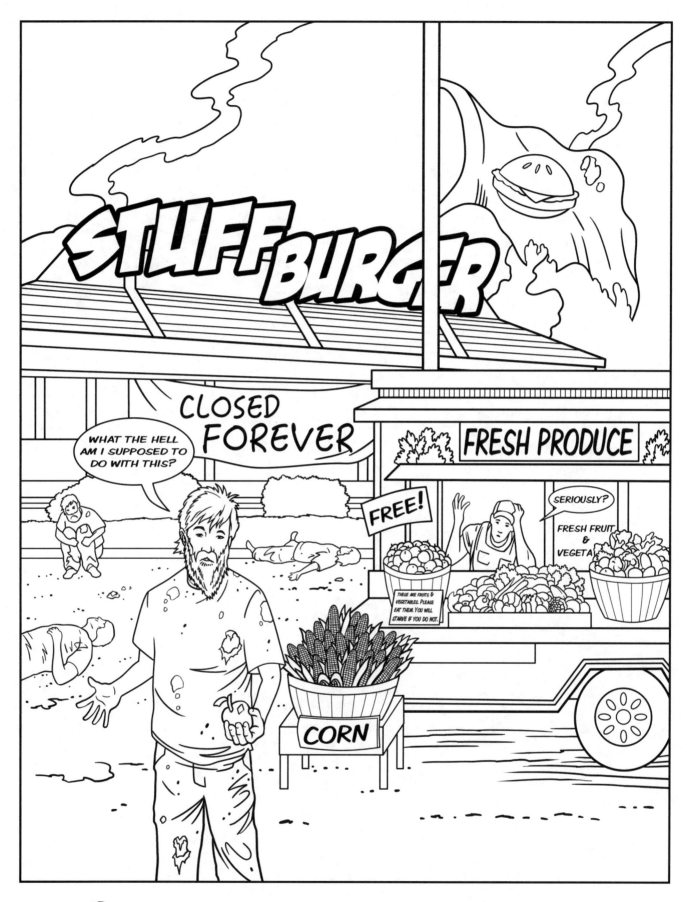

"PART OF THE SECRET OF SUCCESS IN LIFE IS TO EAT WHAT YOU LIKE
AND LET THE FOOD FIGHT IT OUT INSIDE."—MARK TWAIN

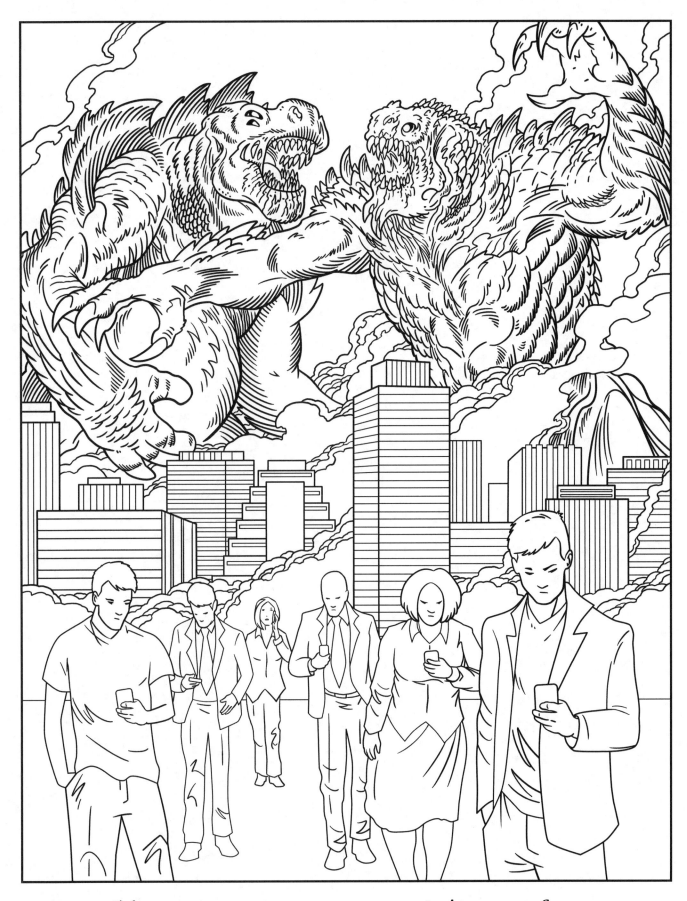

"MAY YOU LIVE EVERY DAY OF YOUR LIFE." —JONATHAN SWIFT

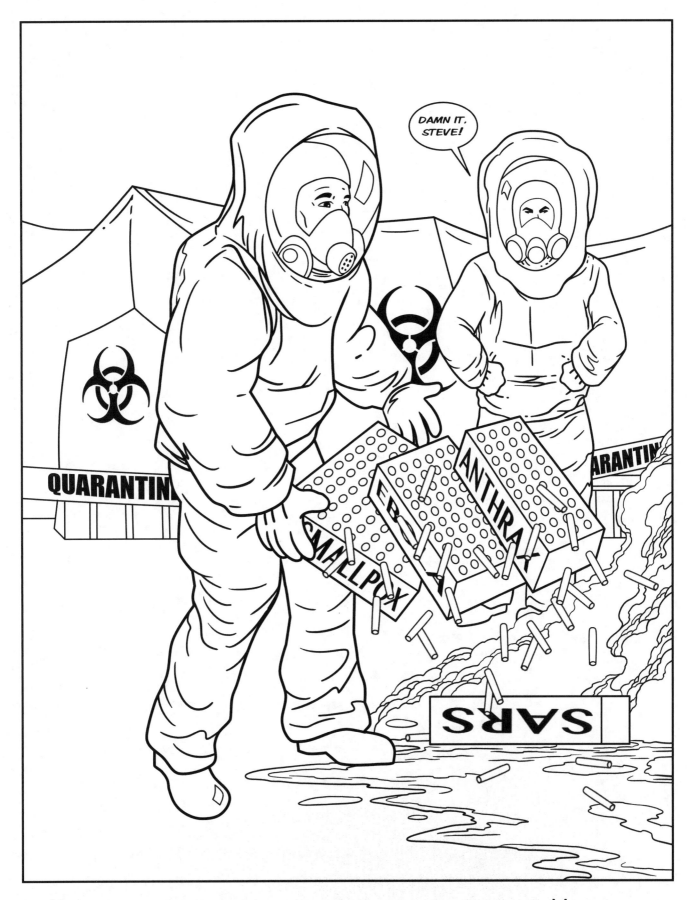

"Natural forces within us are the true healers of disease."—Hippocrates

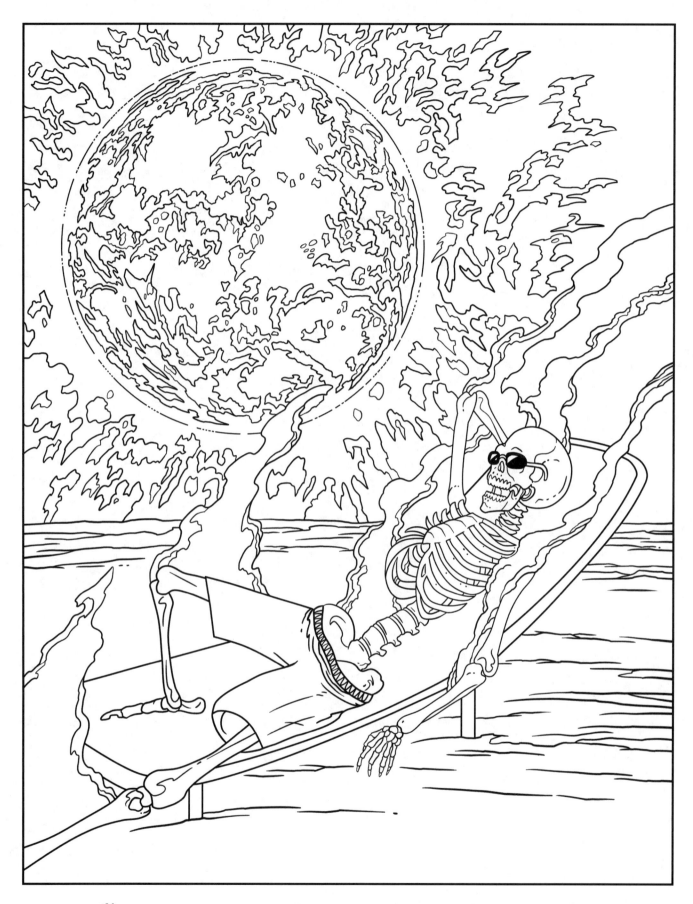

"KEEP YOUR FACE ALWAYS TOWARD THE SUNSHINE—AND SHADOWS
WILL FALL BEHIND YOU."—WALT WHITMAN

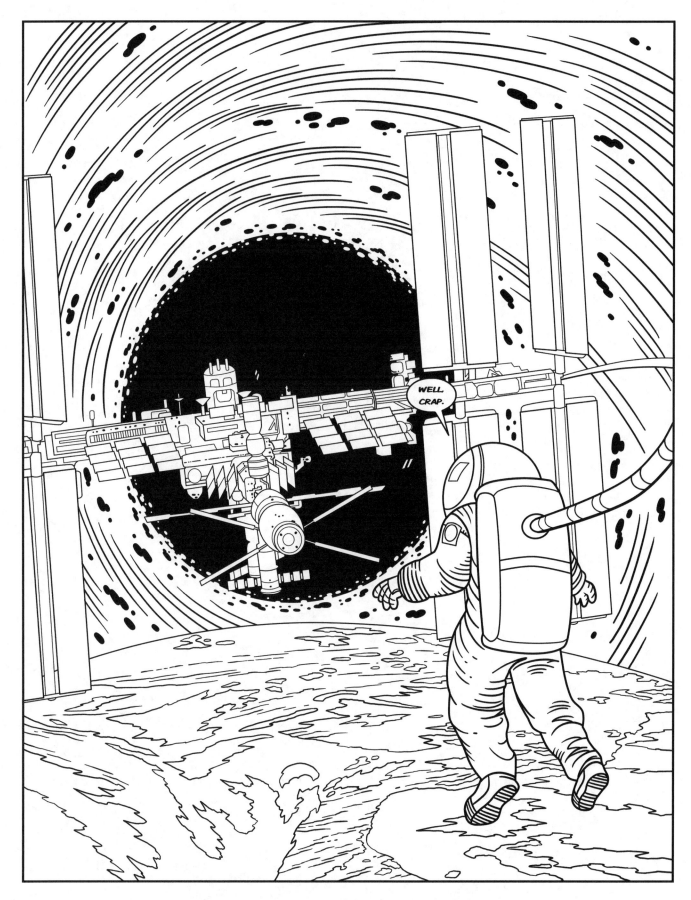

"In three words I can sum up everything
I've learned about life: it goes on." —Robert Frost

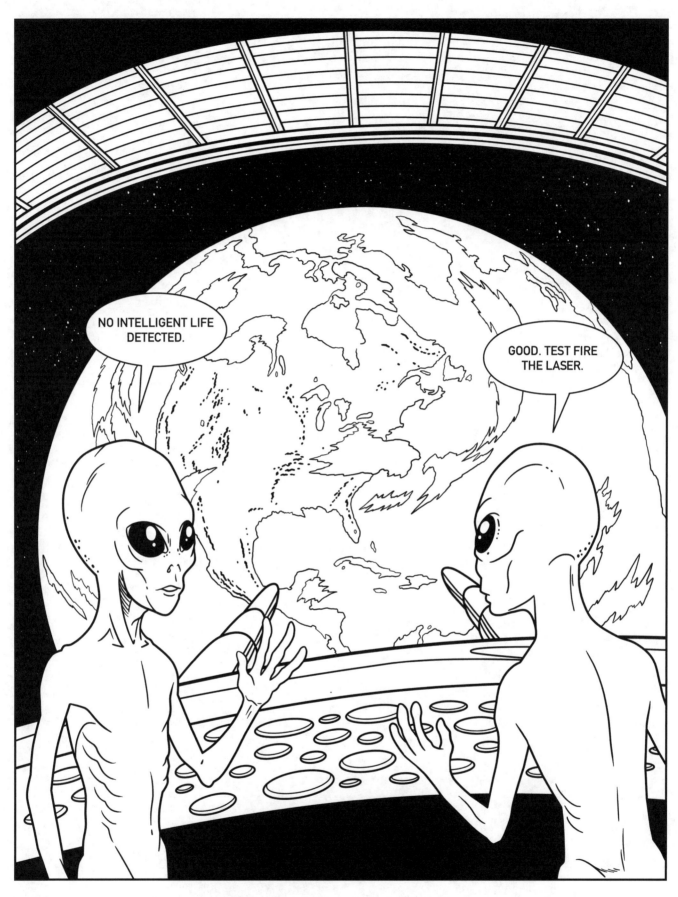

"WE ARE ALL IN THE GUTTER,
BUT SOME OF US ARE LOOKING AT THE STARS."—OSCAR WILDE

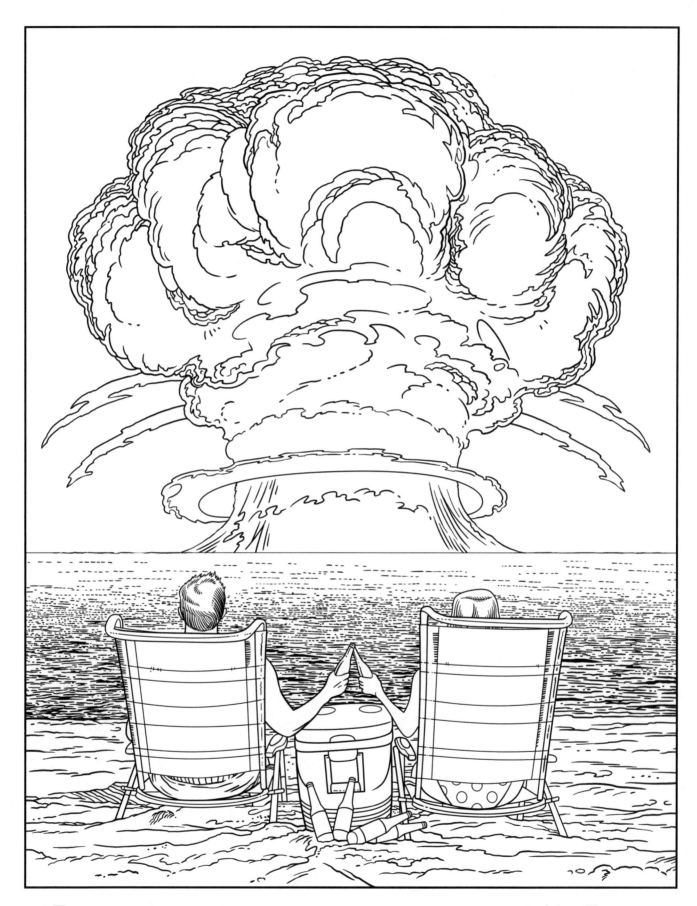

"The two most powerful warriors are patience and time."—Leo Tolstoy

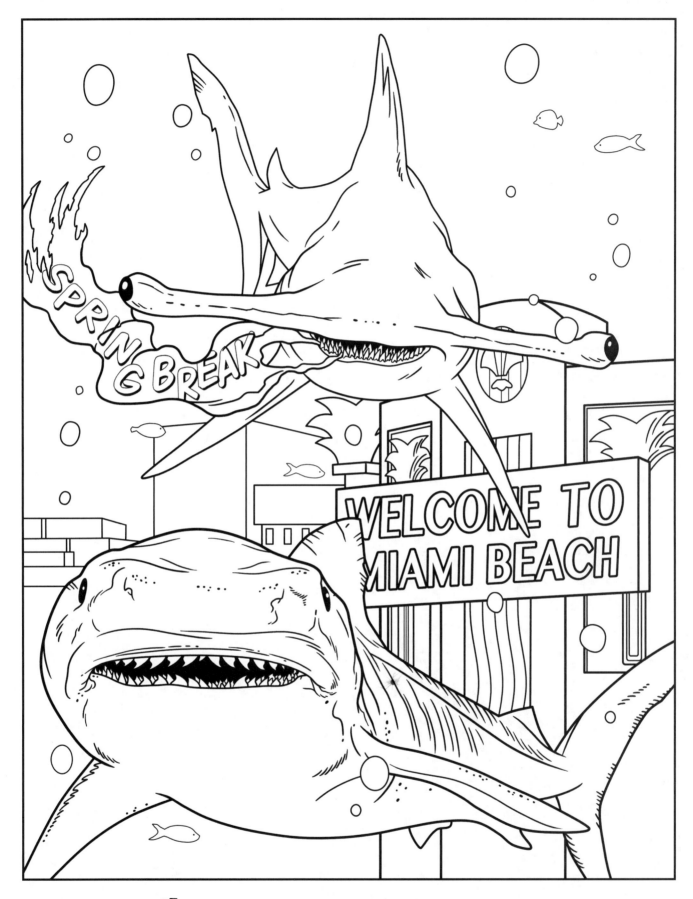

"For whatever we lose (like a you or a me),
it's always ourselves we find in the sea."—E. E. Cummings

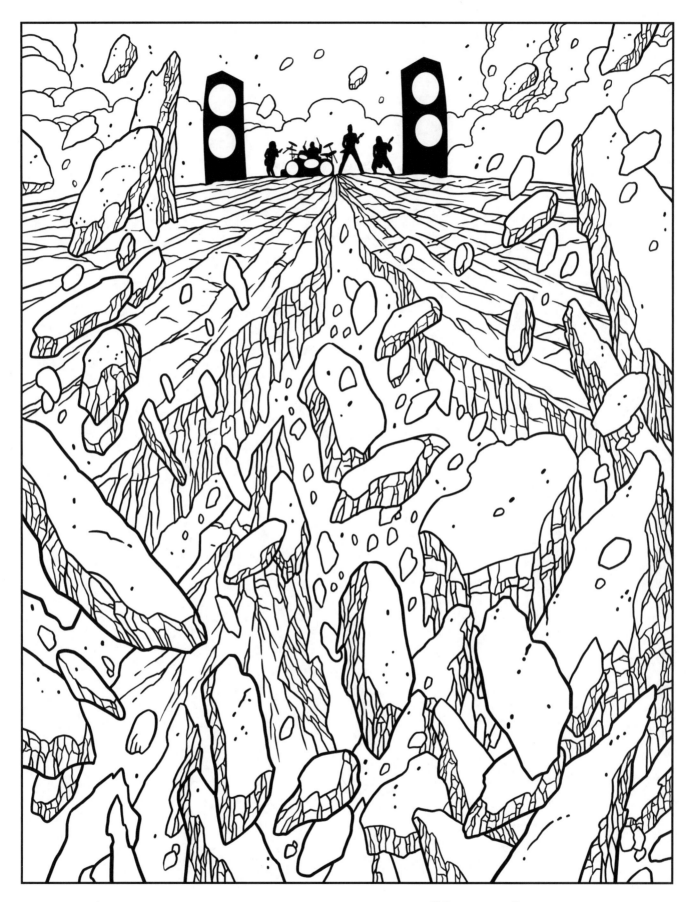

"If music be the food of love, play on."—William Shakespeare

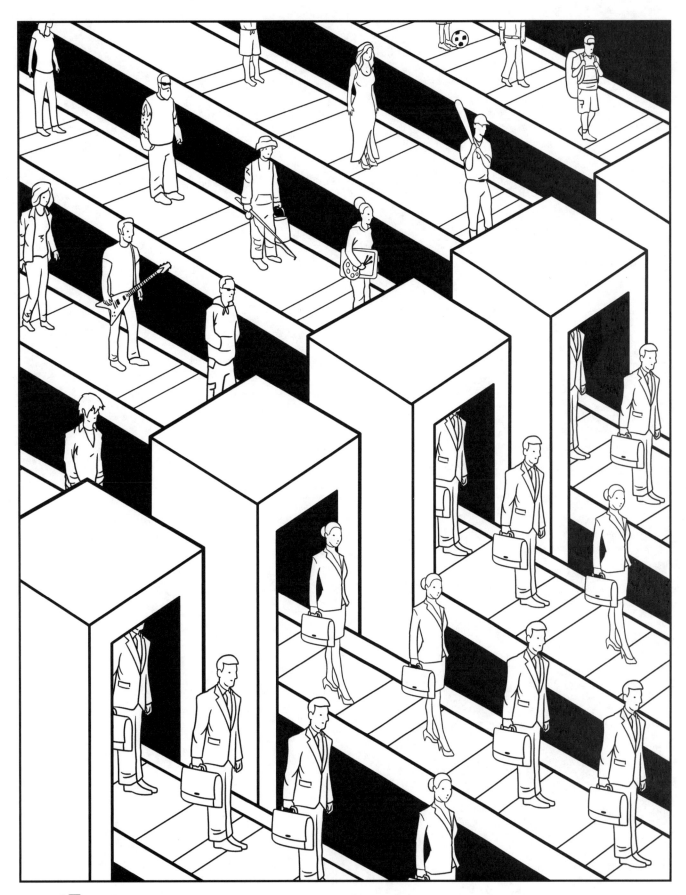

"To be yourself in a world that is constantly trying to make you something else is the greatest accomplishment."—Ralph Waldo Emerson

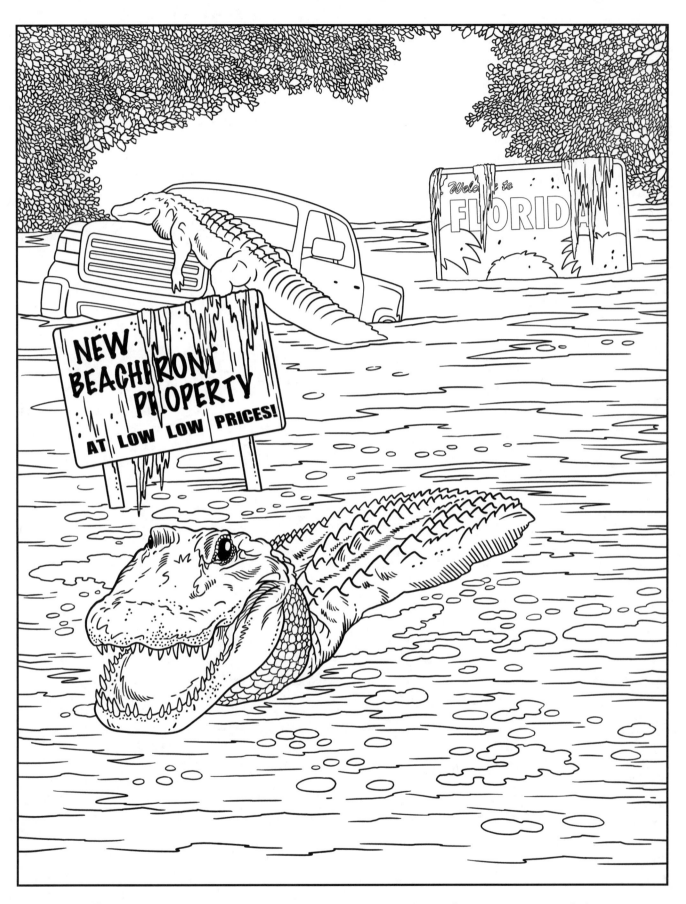

"Water is the driving force of all nature."—Leonardo da Vinci

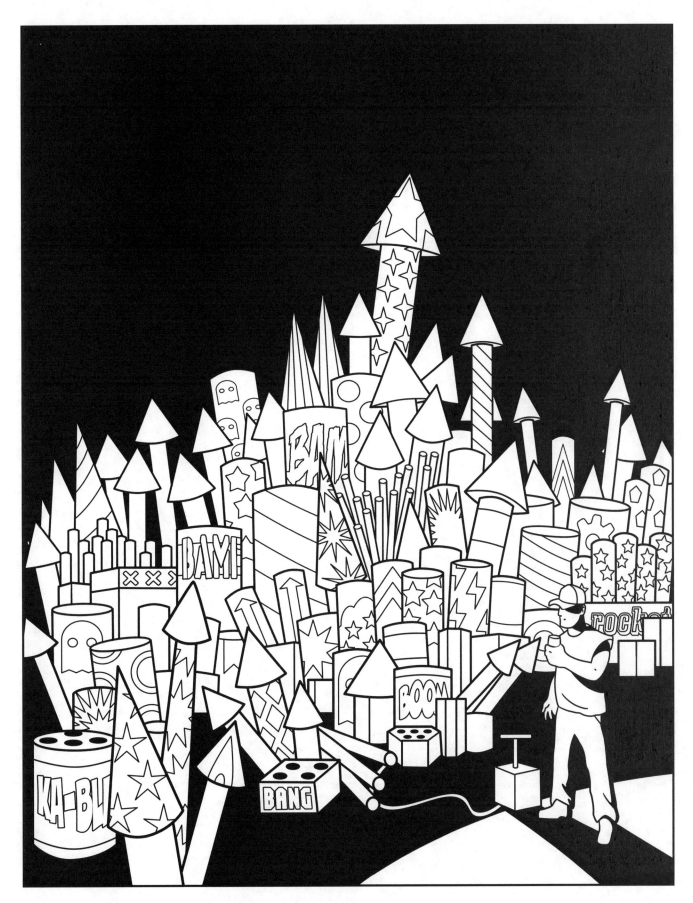

"Light tomorrow with today!"—Elizabeth Barrett Browning

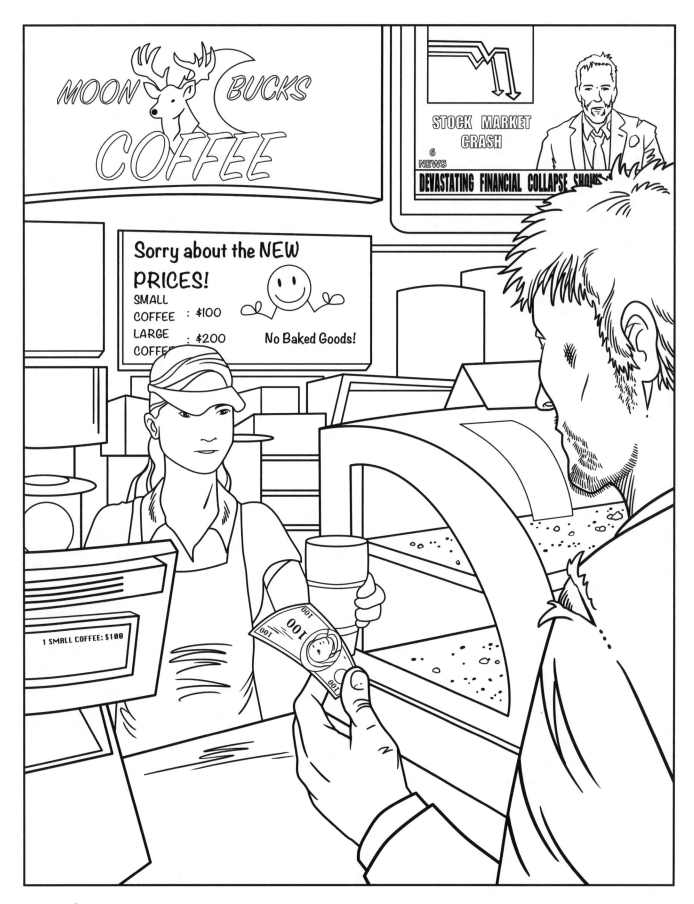

"JUST AS OTHER CLOUDS HAVE CLEARED AWAY IN DUE TIME, SO WILL THIS, AND THIS GREAT NATION SHALL CONTINUE TO PROSPER AS BEFORE."—ABRAHAM LINCOLN

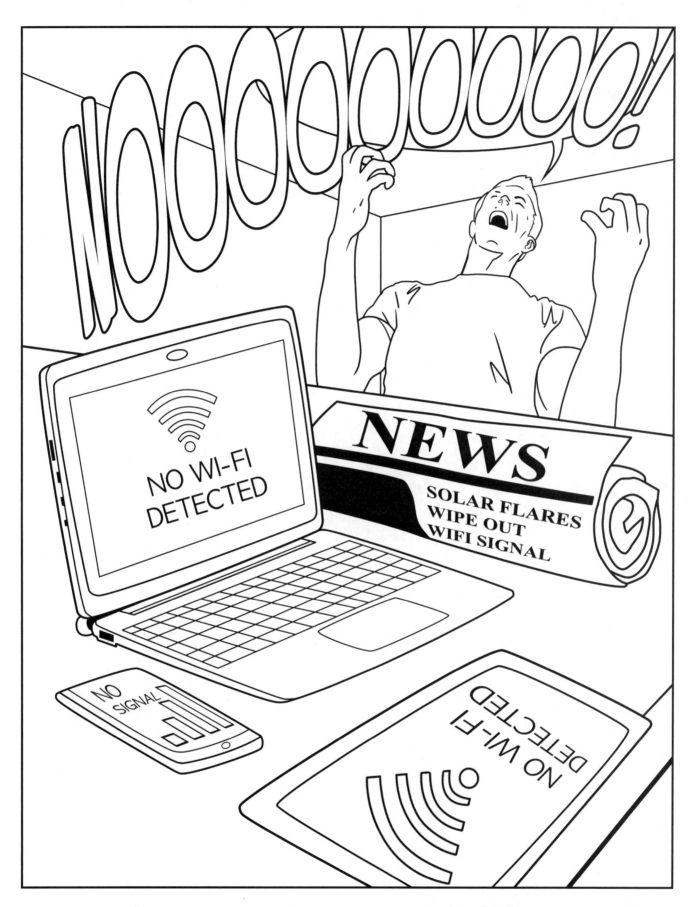

"I HAVE NOT FAILED. I HAVE JUST FOUND 10,000 WAYS
THAT WON'T WORK."–THOMAS EDISON

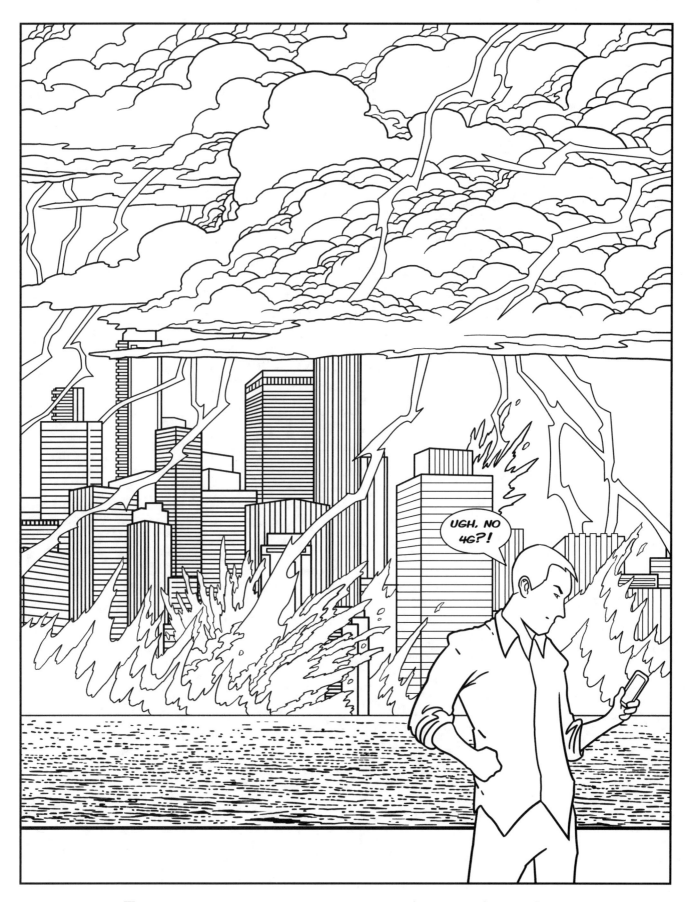

"THERE IS PEACE EVEN IN THE STORM."—VINCENT VAN GOGH

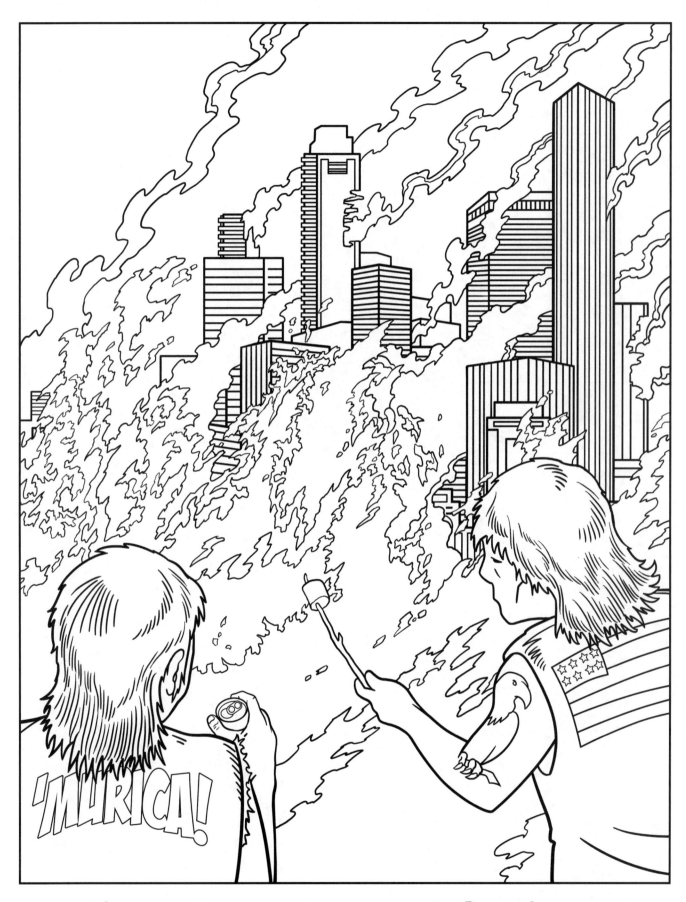

"A mighty flame followeth a tiny spark."—Dante Alighieri

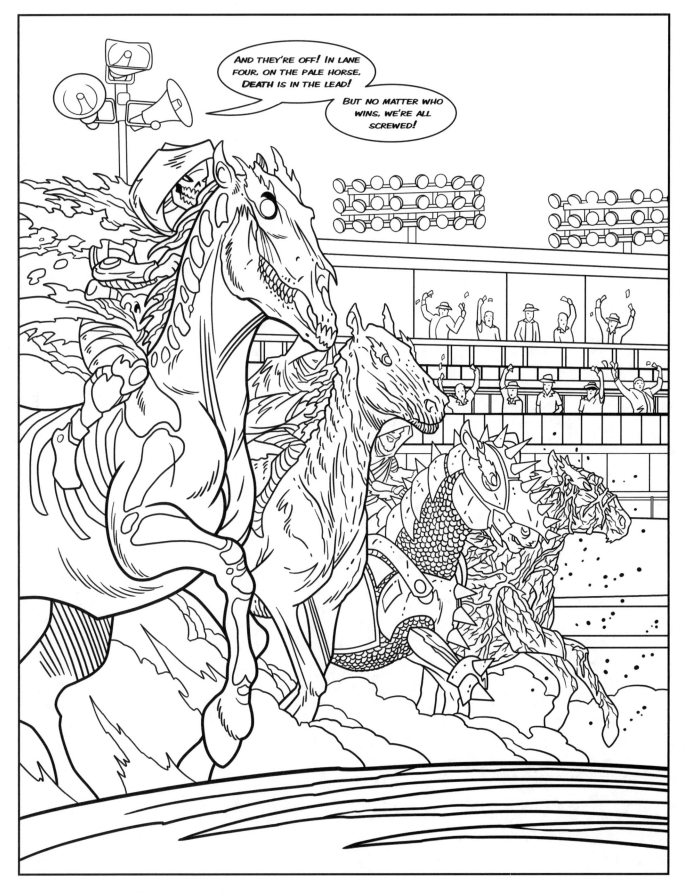

"ENJOY LIFE. THERE'S PLENTY OF TIME TO BE DEAD."—HANS CHRISTIAN ANDERSEN

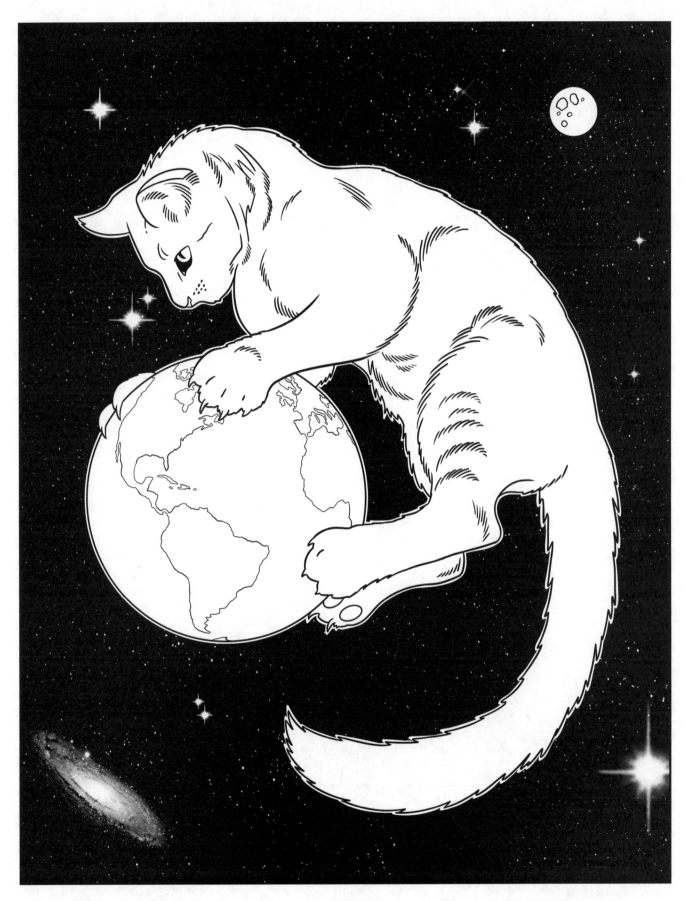

"WHAT GREATER GIFT THAN THE LOVE OF A CAT."—CHARLES DICKENS

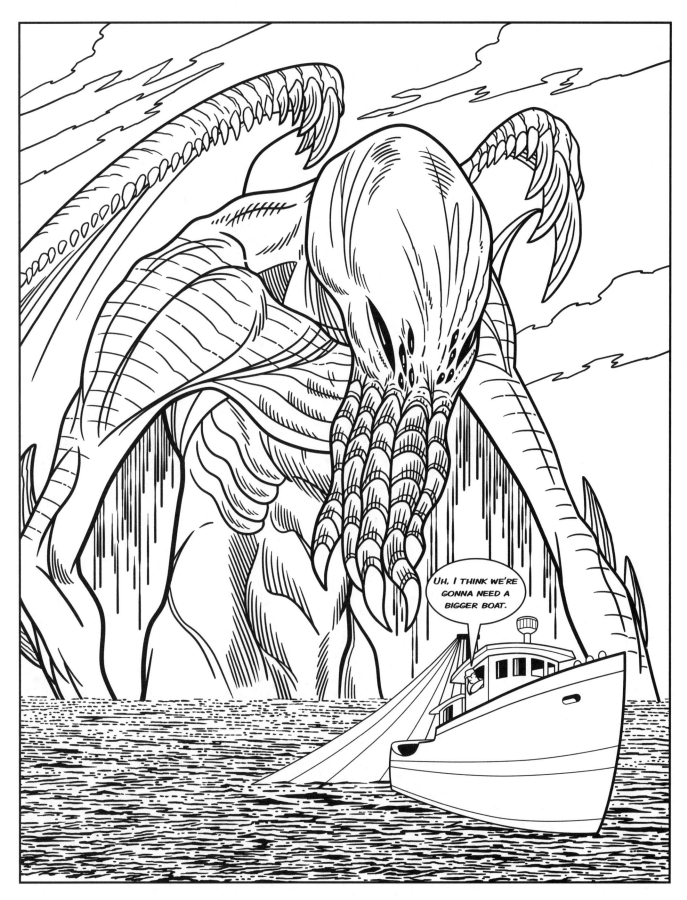

"A thing of beauty is a joy forever." —John Keats

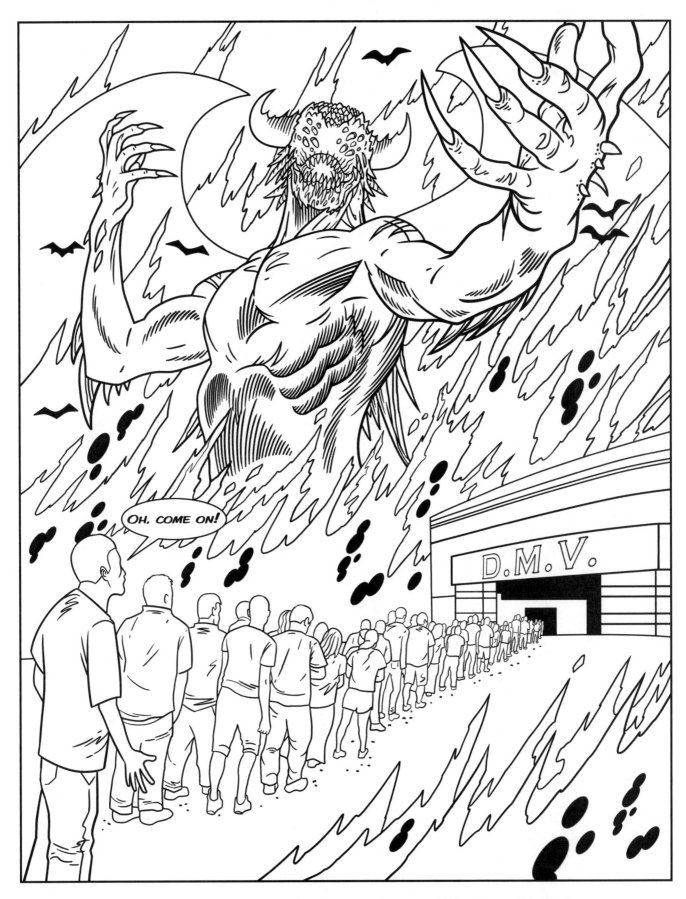

"If you're going through hell, keep going." —Winston S. Churchill

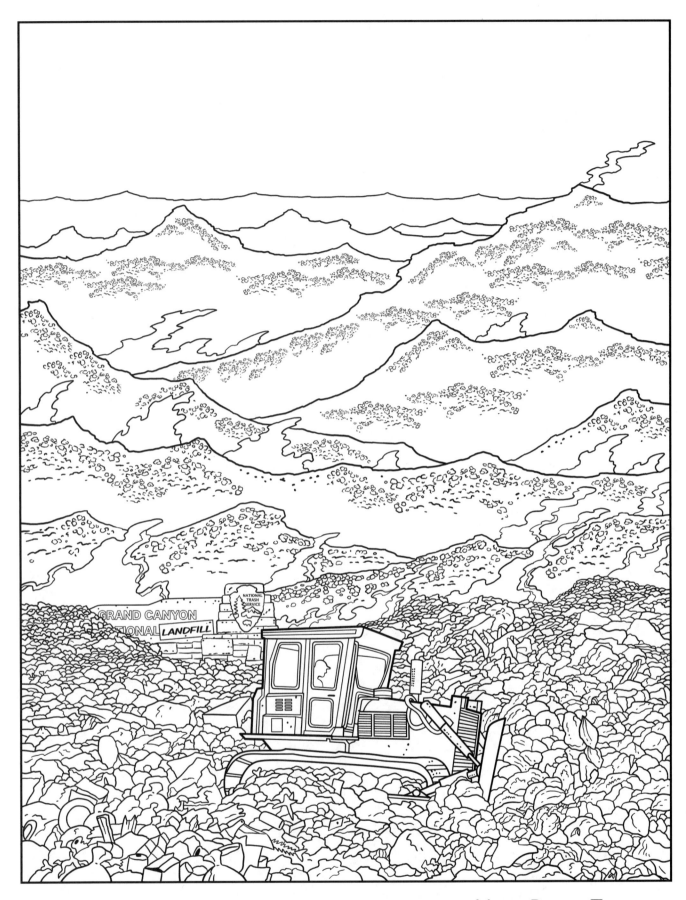

"THIS WORLD IS BUT A CANVAS TO OUR IMAGINATION." —HENRY DAVID THOREAU

PALETTE BARS

Use these bars to test your coloring medium and palette. Don't be afraid to try unique color combinations!

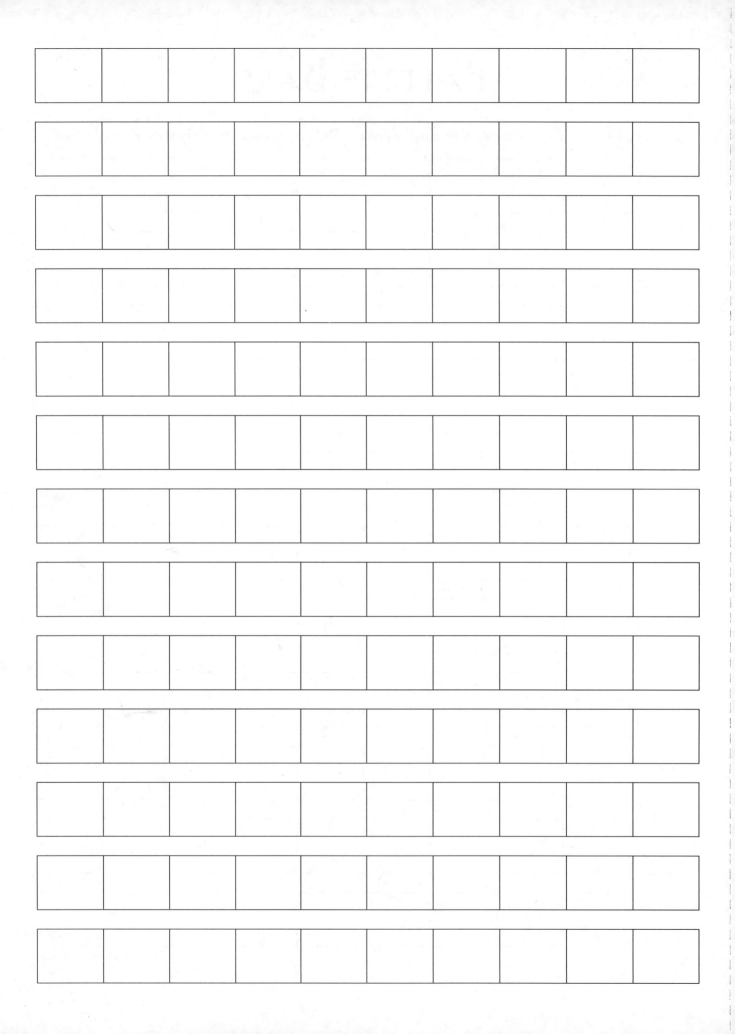